# INTRODUCTION

A lot of animals are up all day and sleep at night—just like you! But there are many animals that rest and sleep during the day. They are active at night instead. These daytime sleepers are called **nocturnal** animals. Some keep a very strict nighttime schedule. But others may sometimes be active during the day, too. Turn the page to meet these nighttime babies!

# LEOPARD

The leopard is one of the smallest of the big cats. These animals are found in Africa, Asia, and India. At birth, a leopard cub is only one or two pounds. But it will grow to be much bigger! At a very young age, leopard cubs learn to chase, **stalk**, and pounce. These skills make them great nighttime hunters when they are older.

A leopard's spots are called rosettes because of their rose shape.

# GREAT HORNED OWL

The great horned owl is found all over North and South America. At birth, an owlet weighs only about one ounce. But the bird can grow up to five and a half pounds. Great horned owls are awesome nocturnal **predators**. They have giant eyes that help them see in near darkness. Their incredible hearing also helps guide them toward **prey**. And their fluffy feathers make them nearly silent while flying.

Great horned owls can carry animals several times their own size!

# BANDICOOT

Bandicoots are found throughout Australia. Bandicoots are **marsupials**. That means the baby joeys live in a pouch on their mother's belly. At birth, bandicoots weigh less than a paper clip. They spend up to three months living in their mother's pouch. Bandicoots are known for their pointy snouts—perfect for poking into holes to find underground prey. They also have excellent hearing and a strong sense of smell to help them hunt at night.

A bandicoot's pouch opens at the bottom instead of the top.

# RACCOON

Raccoons are found in North and South America, Europe, and Japan. They can live in forests, the mountains, or even in your own backyard. A raccoon is known for its white face and black eyes. A mother raccoon has about four or five babies at a time. The babies, called kits, only weigh as much as a cell phone, but they can grow up to 35 pounds!

Raccoons have skilled fingers that make it easy for them to turn doorknobs or even open jars.

# KOALA

Koalas are marsupials that live in eucalyptus trees found in Australia. A koala joey is as small as a jelly bean when it is born. Koalas are sleepy animals. Sometimes they sleep for up to 22 hours a day! Koalas need all this rest to help them digest their food. But by nighttime, these guys are ready for some action! They eat up to two and a half pounds of eucalyptus leaves each night.

The leaves they eat give koalas a cough-drop-like smell.

# PYGMY SLOW LORIS

**P**ygmy slow lorises are small **primates** found in Asia. They have special hands and feet that allow them to grip the branches in their treetop homes. Lorises have a special trick to keep them safe—they make a poison from a **gland** on their elbow that they rub on their fur and in their mouths. At birth, a loris weighs only about as much as a golf ball. So sometimes its mother licks her poison onto its fur until it is big enough to protect itself.

Pygmy slow lorises can seem shy because they often cover their faces when they are spotted by predators.

# NORTHERN FUR SEAL

Most northern fur seals are found in the cold waters of the northern Pacific Ocean. The seal pups are about two feet long when they are born. These seals spend about half of their lives at sea. They even sleep in the water! But the seals can use their flat front and back flippers to walk on land, too. The adults often go hunting at night before returning to the shore to feed their babies.

A group of northern fur seals is called a raft.

# TWO-TOED SLOTH

**T**he two-toed sloth spends all of its time in the rain forests of Central and South America. A newborn sloth weighs less than a pound. It travels on its mother's belly when it is young. Sloths are the slowest **mammals** on Earth. The two-toed sloth spends much of its time sleeping—sometimes up to 20 hours a day! At night, when they are awake, two-toed sloths eat fruits and leaves from nearby trees.

The two-toed sloth does everything hanging upside down—even eating and sleeping!

# TARSIER

Tarsiers are found on islands off the coast of Southeast Asia. At birth, a tarsier is only a couple of inches long. They might be small, but tarsiers learn how to climb trees the day they are born! The tarsier has huge eyes that help it see in the dark. Its eyes are so big that it cannot rotate them. Instead, the tarsier moves its head all the way around to see when it hunts at night.

Tarsiers have powerful legs—some can leap over 16 feet!

# WOMBAT

Wombats are short, round marsupials found in Australia. A wombat joey is no bigger than a coffee bean when it is born. Wombats use their long claws to dig holes and winding, underground tunnels. They live in these tunnels during the day and spend their nighttime eating things like grasses and roots. During the winter, the wombats may even spend some of the daylight hours out of their tunnels.

Scientists believe that wombats had **relatives** the size of rhinos during the Ice Age.

# WHITE RHINO

White rhinos live in the sunny African plains. It is very hot, so the rhinos spend their days hiding in the shade and rolling in mud to keep cool. At birth, a rhino calf can weigh almost as much as an adult human. Its mother uses her long horn to protect her baby for about three years. When the rhino grows its own horn, it is ready to be on its own.

**A white rhino's horn can grow up to three feet long!**

# LITTLE BROWN BAT

Little brown bats are found in caves and wooded areas in North America. A little brown bat pup can fit in your hand. But it is fully grown in about one month. These bats **hibernate** during the winter. In the summer, they sleep together in **roosts** all day. At night, the bats use **echolocation** to find their prey.

The oldest little brown bat was over 30 years old!

# VIRGINIA OPOSSUM

Virginia opossums are the only kind of marsupials found in North America. Newborn opossums are no bigger than bees. They spend lots of time in their mothers' pouches and on their backs until they are big enough to hunt on their own. Opossums will eat almost anything—fruit, birds, snakes, insects, and whatever they can find in your garbage can!

Opossums lie on their sides and play dead when a predator is nearby.

# AARDVARK

Aardvarks are strange-looking animals found throughout Africa. A newborn aardvark is wrinkly and pink and weighs about four pounds. During the day, aardvarks live in burrows underground to hide from the hot African heat. At night they use their sharp claws to dig in the ground for their favorite food—termites! Once an aardvark has dug far enough, it will dip its sticky, pointy tongue into the ground to find its prey.

An aardvark can eat up to 50,000 insects in one night!

# GLOSSARY

**echolocation:** to find objects by sending out sounds and listening for the echoes that bounce back

**gland:** an organ in the body that makes or releases natural chemicals

**hibernate:** to sleep for the entire winter

**mammal:** a warm-blooded animal that has hair or fur and usually gives birth to live babies

**marsupial:** an animal known for the pouch on the mother's belly, where she carries her babies

**nocturnal:** active at night

**predator:** an animal that hunts other animals for food

**prey:** an animal that is hunted by another animal for food

**primate:** any member of the group of mammals that includes (among others) monkeys, apes, and humans

**relative:** a family member

**roost:** a place where winged animals, especially birds or bats, rest or sleep

**stalk**: to hunt or track in a quiet, secret way